metta

metta

The Practice of Loving Kindness

WINDHORSE PUBLICATIONS

Published by
Windhorse Publications
11 Park Road
Birmingham, B13 8AB
email: info@windhorsepublications.com
web: www.windhorsepublications.com

© Windhorse Publications 1992 & 2000
Reprinted 2003

Printed by
Gopsons, India

Cover design Annie Moss
Cover photo Photodisc

British Library Cataloguing in Publication Data:
A catalogue record for this book is available
from the British Library
ISBN 0 904766 99 3

The passages from the *Karaniya Metta Sutta*
on pages 4, 52, and 63–4 are from a free
translation by Ratnaprabha.

Since this work is intended for a general readership,
Pali and Sanskrit words have been transliterated
without the diacritical marks which would have been
appropriate in a work of a more scholarly nature.

Contents

1   About the Contributors

3   Introduction *by Ratnapani*

23 Putting Oneself First *by Abhaya*

29 Opening the Floodgates *by Vidyasri*

36 Breaking Down the Barriers of Prejudice
    by Dhammadinna

44 The Alchemy of Emotion *by Chris Pauling*

50 Opening our Hearts to the World *by Lokamitra*

56 Life, Love, Power, and Violence *by Nagabodhi*

64 The Karaniya Metta Sutta

67 Further Reading

About the Contributors

Ratnapani was ordained in 1973. He has been very involved in the establishment and running of retreat centres within the Friends of the Western Buddhist Order (FWBO), including Padmaloka, a men's retreat centre in Norfolk, England, Aryaloka in New Hampshire, USA, and most recently Vajraloka in Wales. He now lives alone in a cabin on the side of a Welsh mountain.

Abhaya became a member of the Western Buddhist Order (WBO) in 1974. He currently lives in Birmingham, where he is engaged in literary work and teaching for Dharmavastu, the FWBO study centre.

Vidyasri was ordained in 1980 and during the past twenty years has been involved in leading retreats, teaching meditation, and helping women to develop their spiritual practice. She currently lives in Brighton, where she is exploring the potential of ritual and the links between Buddhism and the arts.

Dhammadinna, ordained in 1973, is a senior member of the WBO. She spent ten years teaching Buddhism and meditation in London, and now lives at Tiratanaloka, in

Wales, a retreat centre devoted to helping women to prepare for ordination. She is one of the Public Preceptors of the WBO, who have overall responsibility for those joining the Order.

Chris Pauling lives in Sheffield, England. He has been involved with the FWBO for fifteen years, and wrote the popular *Introducing Buddhism* in 1990. He was ordained in 2000 and given the name Vadanya, 'eloquent'. He currently divides his time between teaching and writing.

Nagabodhi is a senior member of the Western Buddhist Order. Since 1974, when he was ordained, he has devoted his life to the development of the FWBO as a Dharma teacher, writer, publisher, centre director, and fund-raiser. He now lives in Gloucestershire.

Lokamitra is a senior member of the WBO, ordained in January 1974. He spent several years in London teaching meditation and yoga before moving to India in 1977, where he was principally responsible for setting up FWBO activities. He still lives and works for the Movement in India, where it is now known as TBMSG.

Introduction

by Ratnapani

When we look at the life of the Buddha, there is one quality that really shines out, in his actions, in his words, and in his teachings: the quality of kindness. The source of his kindness towards all beings was *metta. Metta* (Pali) or *maitri* (Sanskrit) is a wish for the welfare of other beings, human and non-human, without any self-reference – that is, without wanting or expecting anything in return. In simple language, *metta* is universal loving kindness – with no strings attached.

There are many references in the earliest Buddhist texts to metta and its benefits: the Buddha spoke of the 'radiant brightness' of metta, of the beneficial effect the cultivation of metta can have on one's rebirth, and of the importance of metta as the basis for meditative concentration. In a passage stressing the importance of metta in all situations, the Buddha sums up what we are trying to achieve through the practice of metta:

> There are these five kinds of speech that others may address to you – timely or untimely, true or false, mild

or harsh, profitable or unprofitable, with goodwill or bearing malice.... You should train yourselves, thinking, 'Our minds will not be altered, and we shall not speak evil words, and we shall live friendly and compassionate, with thoughts of goodwill, not bearing malice. And we shall live pervading that person with a mind joined to goodwill, abundantly, boundlessly, unrestrictedly, peaceably, benevolently.' Thus are you to train yourselves.*

Although the importance of metta is stressed in passages such as these, there is less to be found concerning how one should actually develop it. But in the *Karaniya Metta Sutta* we find the following advice:

(Then meditate like this:) May all be happy and feel secure. May all beings become happy in their heart of hearts!... As strongly as a mother, perhaps risking her life, cherishes her child, her only child, develop an unlimited heart for all beings. Develop an unlimited heart of friendliness (metta) for the entire universe, sending metta above, below, and all around, beyond all narrowness, beyond all rivalry, beyond all hatred.

In a scriptural commentary from the fourth century CE by Buddhagosa (a famous commentator of the Theravada tradition of Buddhism) we find a more detailed description of a meditation practice devoted to the development of metta. So we have today the meditation known as the 'Metta Bhavana' – and it is this practice we will be looking at in some detail in this book.

* *Majjhima Nikaya* 21, trans. David W. Evans, in *Discourses of Gotama Buddha, Middle Collection*, Janus, London 1992.

Bhavana is a Pali word meaning development or cultivation, and it is important to note that in these practices, and in this book, we are talking about the *development* of metta. If we already possessed strong metta in all circumstances, for all people, we ourselves would be well on our way to Enlightenment, but most of us are at the stage of gradually exchanging our current experience for one of metta.

So what is our current experience? Do we feel loving kindness? Is it really without self-interest?

The word 'love' is the one we most frequently use for this type of emotion. But 'love' is problematic as a translation of metta, as it often describes a state that is involved primarily with ourselves, with greed. What do we 'love'? Coffee? Travelling? Our mother? Our partner? These 'loves' are often self-referential; we love them for the pleasant sensations they bring us, we like the experience of being close to them, so we move towards them and become attached to them. If these loves of ours are people, we are happy when they behave as we want them to behave, but when they don't we become unhappy and may withdraw our affection. When frustrated in this way, when we no longer get the desired effect from the object of our affection, our emotion can too easily turn to ill will, to anger or hurt or annoyance. So love, as a definition of metta, is a word that needs to be treated with caution.

Closer to metta is the ideal of parental love. Within this ideal, love is never withdrawn, but remains constant, whether correcting or encouraging our child. With metta, too, our response does not depend on whether its recipient behaves in a way that pleases or displeases us. Moreover, with metta this well-wishing extends to all beings, whether we know them or not.

However, we may find that much of our experience is conditional. In response to pleasant experience we feel happy, in the face of unpleasant experience we feel unhappy; we like things that give us pleasure and we dislike things that give us pain. Most of us have very little of what we could call emotional freedom. We react automatically to our shifting likes and dislikes, our loves and hates. We are victims of circumstance and of our conditioning – little more than a ball on the ping-pong table of life.

We do not have to be like this. We can free ourselves from these reactions and gain emotional freedom. Step by step we can gain mastery of our automatic emotional reactions to ourselves, to others, and to the world. We can then have the pleasure of consistently dwelling in more positive states of mind.

The way to that freedom lies in deeper and more lasting forms of positive emotion through the development of metta. With metta we find it possible to achieve a more satisfactory, indeed more human, existence – away from this mutability of our emotions, away from love and hate. In a world composed of a mixture of pleasure and pain, it comes as a relief to realize that we can develop this sort of equanimity.

The premise of the Metta Bhavana meditation is that metta is something that can be practised. We can develop positive and creative responses to those we hate, or those who hate us. Moreover, we can deepen and purify our feelings towards those we already love, and develop warmth towards those whom, as yet, we have no particular feelings. To develop metta, universal loving kindness, may sound a tall order – it is not easy to change our emotional experience all at once – but the effects of the regular cultivation of loving kindness are reliable and cumulative.

Many of us believe, in a vaguely post-Freudian sort of way, that large parts of ourselves are unconscious, and that these parts are probably rather dark and murky. My experience as a meditation teacher is that, on the contrary, much that is not 'on the surface' of our minds is positive. Through the practice of meditation we can sometimes release previously suppressed benevolence and joy. The effects of any one session of the Metta Bhavana may not lead to a dramatic change in our responses, although they may, but we can know that we are, by repetition, creating new and more positive paths in our lives, leaving the old, duller ways behind. Practising the Metta Bhavana regularly, we learn that 'what we dwell upon we become'. Once we've been practising for a while we will naturally tend to develop the attitudes and ideals engendered by metta outside meditation, no longer sitting on our cushion. In this way the metta practice will improve the quality of our emotional life in general.

The positive states that liberate us (and others) from the bondage of automatic reactions are all those that are free of ill will, greed, and confusion; for example, friendliness, kindness, generosity, appreciation, and compassion. We have seen that one characteristic of the experience of metta is that it demands nothing in return. With time, or a change of circumstances, it does not tip over into ill will, possessiveness, jealousy, or boredom. Instead, it is expansive, light, warm, and unrestricted. If our heart, and, indeed, our consciousness, feels as though it is expanding, we are probably on the right track.

In performing the practice we do not have to worry about consciously eliminating considerations of self. Rather, as metta grows, we will naturally expand out of our hard shell of self-reference. With metta, we wish others well for their own sake, not for our own. Through the practice of Metta Bhavana, relationships with those we love, those we hate, and with the many for whom we feel something in between, can be completely transformed. In the words of the Buddha:

> From where should anger arise for him who,
>   void of anger,
> Holds on the even tenor of his way.
> Self-tamed, serene, by highest insight free?
> Worse of the two is he who, when reviled,
> Reviles in turn. Who does not, when reviled,
> Revile in turn, a twofold victory wins,
> Both of the other and himself he seeks
> The good; for he the other's angry mood

Understands and has mindfulness and calm.
He of both is a physician, since
Himself he heals and the other too.*

Metta in its fullest sense, as we have seen, is loving
kindness for *all*. In our meditation we will naturally feel
metta for many different kinds of people in many different situations, and the emotion will take on different
nuances accordingly. Towards someone who is suffering,
for example, we feel a kind of metta that includes a desire
for the alleviation of their suffering. This is compassion
(*karuna*). We may or may not be able to help them
physically, but we will at least be engaged with that
person in a healthy emotional way. On the other hand,
when someone is fortunate metta will take the form of
sympathetic joy (*mudita*); we are happy that they are
happy, and with that there is an end to jealousy – what
joy! And then there is equanimity (*upekkha*) which is
metta conjoined with clarity. This is the clarity that
comes when we are confronted with reality, when we see
how things really are in this world: how people constantly
experience pleasure followed by pain. And we see something of what brings this about, especially through the
laws of karma. If we also have metta conjoined with this
clarity, our experience is equanimity; not optimism, nor
pessimism, nor fatalism, but equanimity: metta pervading
a sense of the true nature of things. These four: metta,
karuna, mudita, and upekkha are known as the four

* Adapted from *Samyutta-Nikaya* i.162, trans. C.A.F. Rhys Davids as *Book of
the Kindred Sayings*, Pali Text Society, London 1950.

brahma viharas or 'sublime abodes', and it is quite true that if we diligently practise the Metta Bhavana our life will become increasingly sublime.

PREPARATION

Preparation for any meditation practice is very important, but this is especially so in the case of the Metta Bhavana. The obvious place to start is with our body. Awareness of our body gives our practice a firm foundation. The body is also a link with the emotions; we can often feel our emotions – or learn to recognize their signs – within our body, and we can work on transforming our emotions there, rather than in our head. For example, we may recognize that our tension is caused by ill will, and that by releasing that tension we can help dissolve that ill will, or we can experiment with physically 'letting go' into the expansiveness of metta. By maintaining our bodily awareness we can maintain our focus on our heart centre, and work through the sensations we discover within to develop and adjust our practice.

When we are aware how our body is feeling, we can turn our attention to our general level of energy and our specific emotional states. Both of these help us to know our starting point. This is important, since we can only really work effectively from 'where we are at' rather than from where we would like to be. If we are working from some imaginary state, of what we would prefer to be feeling, the practice tends to be as though on a piece of elastic – we can superimpose some metta upon our experience, or force some metta to the fore (or more likely only an idea of metta), but the experience will be unstable and will snap back. If, however, we are working from wherever we really are, no matter how seemingly negative, it is possible to develop the constituents of metta bit by bit, and so cultivate it genuinely and spontaneously.

There are four qualities that can help us set up the right conditions for our meditation and assist us during the practice. The first constituent we need is contentment. If you are not content to sit on your cushion you are not going to get very far. So we can check: do we feel content? If we do, we can focus on and encourage that feeling. If we do not, we can spend a little time finding the causes of our discontent and perhaps overcome them, or simply encourage ourselves to relax and be at ease.

Having established a degree of contentment we consider confidence. 'Am I confident that I can do this practice, that I can develop metta?' If so, fine, encourage that feeling. If not, we can take steps to develop confidence, reminding ourselves, 'I have done this before. I can do it again, even if the circumstances are less conducive.' Similarly, we can recall a time when we felt kind or expansive. Perhaps we lack confidence in the practice itself. If so, we can reflect that innumerable people have successfully practised the Metta Bhavana, that the Buddha himself recommended it, and so on. For some people just bringing to mind the word 'confidence' will encourage that experience, for others, using an image that conjures up confidence may also work.

Thirdly, we need enthusiasm in order to practise meditation. Without it, our practice will all too readily become dull, and we will slip into the habit of a rather vague effort. When we contact and develop enthusiasm, we are also encouraging and strengthening our positive volitions. Reflecting on the benefits gained from previous practice, and the potential that is yet to be realized, will help our enthusiasm. Traditionally, the benefits are said to be a clear demeanour: sleeping well, with pleasant dreams, and being popular and easily liked. Many people who practise this meditation report improved physical and psychological health.

Now, with the fourth quality, we are ready to take the first steps into metta itself by developing the quality of kindness. Starting with a general sense of kindness eases us into the practice, and avoids the tendency to try to go straight for a powerful experience. Is there a feeling of benevolence towards ourselves and other people that we could bring to mind? It is worth taking this initial step, because it results in a pliability of mind that allows the practice to be more effective. If kindness isn't present, the mind will be tight and our efforts will fall on stony ground.

It is worth taking as long as necessary to establish these four qualities of mind – contentment, confidence, enthusiasm, and kindness – before starting the first stage of the practice. It is arguably better to spend thirty minutes getting into a generally positive state, followed by ten in the development of some real metta, than forty minutes struggling with an unconvincing emotional experience. Not that all this should be dismissed as 'just' preparation: if we are developing positive states of mind, we are doing the meditation.

THE MEDITATION PRACTICE

The Metta Bhavana itself is divided into five stages, five or ten minutes being devoted to each. In these stages we bring to mind, in turn, ourselves, a good friend, a 'neutral' person, an 'enemy' or difficult person, and finally all sentient beings. For each person in the first four stages we first contact, and then develop, feelings of kindness and friendliness – quite independently of any of our usual, automatic, conditioned reactions. In the fifth stage we direct those feelings towards all four persons equally, and then slowly expand our frame of reference, and our hearts, to include all beings everywhere.

Other chapters in this book include suggestions to help with the cultivation of metta in each of the stages, so in this introduction we will look at each stage with particular reference to the way in which we can go beyond our usual limited responses to pleasure and pain, and our likes and dislikes.

To start with, we need to be clear what we should be doing. Our aim is not to try to develop pleasant feelings and merely to feel good about other people. These are feelings that just stay within us. Rather, we actively wish that other people be well – whether we feel good about them or not. We are developing an emotion that flows out of us, not one that remains within: an emotion that contains warmth and interest in other beings.

It is useful to reflect on the good qualities of others, or ourselves, during the meditation, as this will encourage the mudita described above. But we need to avoid the temptation to settle for nice, comfortable feelings that are based on personal gratification, or trying to make our disliking change into liking as a prerequisite of metta. These feelings keep us within our limited automatic reactions of liking and disliking, pleasure and pain, which are based on self-reference. We will now look briefly at each stage in turn.

In the first stage we develop metta *towards* ourselves. The development of metta is a necessary first step if we find that our attitude towards ourselves is not at all kind or appreciative. There may be aspects of ourselves of which we are quite reasonably ashamed – a lack of generosity, a short temper, or a tendency to lie. This sort of objective assessment of ourselves is not antithetical to the development of metta – awareness of our short-comings or faults is no reason not to feel a sense of well-wishing and kindness towards ourselves, just as it is no reason not to feel it for others. Indeed, one might reflect that the greater our faults, which are based on negative emotions, the greater the urgency to develop positive emotions to free us from the mental states that lead us to act unkindly or unhelpfully. We can, of course, also reflect on all our positive qualities and develop a healthy self-appreciation, being careful to discriminate between real self-mudita, rejoicing in our positive qualities, and mere cosy feelings.

In addition to this, we can also try to inculcate a state of metta *within* ourselves; we can pervade ourselves with the feelings of metta. Having rolled away, at least to some degree and for a short while, unhelpful self-views, we can encourage feelings of benevolence to permeate our consciousness. During this stage we move from sustained thoughts and understanding of metta, to a change of heart. We could think to ourselves, 'May I be happy,' as a subtle thought, to suffuse our being with positivity. Just an imaginative 'opening up' will suffice to fill us with the warmth of metta.

In the second stage of the meditation we focus on a good friend. This stage is arguably the easiest, since a positive feeling is already present towards those we call our friends. However, it can also reveal interesting areas of attachment and expectation. For instance, how do we respond if our friend doesn't keep in contact with us? If we feel metta for them it will be sustained – even when we are not 'getting' anything from them. If we are hurt or disappointed and start to feel ill will, we are still to some extent stuck within self-reference. Similarly, what if they do or say something to hurt us? Does our level of metta plummet? This is an interesting exercise for an experienced practitioner of the Metta Bhavana. Metta is not limited by time and space, but bears absent people in mind and keeps the affection alive. Having established yourself in the second stage of the practice you can imagine your friend behaving in different ways. Firstly, doing something which you would applaud, then something 'neutral' like walking down a street, and then doing something of which you would disapprove. Carefully observe your response to each situation. If the metta varies, then to some degree it is conditioned by your own likes and dislikes, and is therefore not entirely the real thing. If there is no fluctuation in your emotion, then you have got metta.

The 'neutral' person of the third stage is arguably the quintessential subject for the development of metta. We have nothing to gain or to lose – we are not ruled by our likes and dislikes. If our emotion is based on self-reference, we will find it difficult to maintain positive feelings. Obviously, for us, the majority of people are 'neutral' – and it is towards this majority, towards all beings, in fact, that we wish eventually to develop metta. In the absence of self-reference, we have to develop positive feelings based on our common humanity, our empathy for other human beings. We can ask ourselves: does neutrality in terms of likes and dislikes in any way hinder our development of positivity, or can metta flourish simply because the neutral person is a person? We can consider that in the same way we want to be happy, they want to be happy too. As we wish to escape suffering, so too do they.

Just as the development of metta towards a good friend means working with the relationship between metta and pleasure, so in the fourth stage of the meditation the development of metta towards an 'enemy' or someone we find difficult means working with the relationship between metta and pain. If we feel ill will towards, or coming from, another person, we usually experience a degree of pain as part of our automatic reaction. Pain, as we saw in the first stage, in relation to our own short-comings, does not preclude a positive response of metta; we can experience the two together. We can also reflect how, when we experience physical pain, we do not necessarily sink into a negative state of mind. It is exactly the same when we experience emotional pain. When we are bruised or hurt we can still maintain and develop a positive state of mind, a state of metta.

There is no need to make everything OK in this stage, to persuade yourself that the difficult person is actually nice, and to gloss over the difficulties. Rather, in the very face of these difficulties, we can develop an attitude of kindness and even love. Again, it is worth remembering that the aim is not to feel good simply by imagining that everything is fine between you. You are not necessarily trying to like them or feel good about what they have done, but wishing them freedom from their suffering and seeing that what they are doing is their own suffering.

Before considering the fifth stage of the practice, it is worth looking at some areas that pertain to all the stages. All meditation practices involve focusing attention on an object. This is true of the Metta Bhavana, but what that object is can be misunderstood. In each of the first four stages of the practice we are developing metta towards a particular person, and as part of that process we will be trying to visualize, or experience, that person as clearly as we can. It is important that we keep them in mind and to be sure that we are responding to them rather than to ourselves. If not, if we become disengaged from that person, our emotion will become subjective and not an active wish for their well-being. However, we also need to maintain awareness of our emotional response to that person, as it is that response that we are working to change through our meditation.

So we will have the people we are bringing to mind as one important focus, but we are primarily working to create greater and greater degrees of positive emotion. The more we concentrate on the emotion, the more it will grow. If it is not growing, we will become aware of this and, if our concentration on our emotional centre is clear enough, we will even become aware what is getting in our way. If the focus of our attention is entirely on the person, and as a consequence we are less clear about what we are actually feeling, we may well find we have a tendency to direct only an *idea* of metta towards that person – rather than an experience of it.

Having an idea about an emotion rather than the emotion itself is not uncommon. We can get stuck in an idea of how we *should* be feeling rather than experiencing *what* we are feeling, so it is often worth asking oneself 'What do I actually feel?' and waiting to see what we experience. Cultivating a state of metta within is a gentle exercise, and what we feel may not be very powerful – though it can be of course. What is important is to be open to our heart, rather than drowned in ideas about the person on whom we focus. Whether the answer to the question is 'deep and glorious metta' or 'not a lot', it is best to know, and work from there.

We run up against the limitations of language here, too, as some of the words we must use to describe the practice do not always help. 'Directing' metta towards someone can be rather too concrete a metaphor. It can encourage us to pump up a feeling through thought and then 'squirt' it at our chosen person. And what we would then be 'squirting' would be as much an idea as genuine friend-liness. This idea can lead us to try to force out an inappropriate emotion rather than working from the basis of our present experience – whatever that is. If we are in a negative state we can work on building basic positivity. If we have a gentle experience of metta, we can let that flow out softly. If there is a strong experience we can allow it to pour out. Here lies the advantage of an attitude of developing an experience of metta 'within and around' ourselves, a state of metta, and then introducing each person into that.

Now for the fifth stage of the meditation. In a way, this is Metta Bhavana proper, the practice in its fullness, and certainly its culmination, for in the Pali descriptions of Metta Bhavana it occupies more space than the other stages. The object of the Metta Bhavana is to develop metta towards all beings. You could see the four preceding stages as practising on different sorts of beings in preparation for this last stage. In this stage we start by putting all four people from the earlier stages together, and seeing how a variety of ordinary responses can be transformed into one emotion – metta. We practise equalizing our emotional response to all four: ourselves, a friend, a neutral person, and an enemy, and only when there is no variation in metta towards all four, when we have dropped all self-reference, is there metta in its fullest sense.

This is a wonderful prospect just to contemplate: to feel friendliness, even love, towards all sentient beings, to say nothing of the experience itself. This experience, in its fullness, is one of a strong and equal positive regard for all beings everywhere. It is the experience of an enlightened one, a Buddha – which says a lot for the potential of the practice. Meanwhile, we can have a temporary experience of this stage of metta, but we must be careful that the very loftiness of the ideal does not lead us to strain ourselves whilst we are still on the nursery slopes of the mountain of metta. We may be in danger of concluding that metta is necessarily a powerful experience, and fail to recognize it in its quieter forms. This may lead us to an attitude of wanting to get right away from our present emotional state and straight into a different, more desirable, experience. We need to guard against this and take care that we start with our present emotional experience, whatever it is. This will include those positive qualities we have developed in the course of the practice so far, but may also include less desirable elements, such as 'who cares about them all anyway'. All this needs to be taken into account.

In all stages of the meditation, having the heart as an important focus of our attention helps make us aware of the first stirrings of our emotions. So we do not, for instance, think 'May they be happy,' so often and so loudly that it drowns out whatever response there is in our heart. Better to say the words, or whatever method of cultivation one is using, then pause to see if there is a response, and of what that response consists. Although not strong or dramatic the metta might nevertheless be present and real, ready to be encouraged and developed.

In the same vein, perhaps, one hears the Metta Bhavana practice described as 'the development of universal loving kindness' and we might be discouraged at the prospect of needing to develop some sort of experience that encompasses the whole universe. This may be where the minds of advanced beings start, but if we are daunted by numbers we are probably better advised to take 'universal' as meaning 'each one equally'. We can develop a steady and thorough feeling of metta into which we can introduce as many people as possible. The gradual expansion of the number of beings can then develop the strength of the metta, rather than thin it out in order to 'make it go round'.

But what if the practice runs dry at some point? If we lose contact with metta at any time it is as well to set ourselves up again as described earlier – with contentment, confidence, enthusiasm, and kindness. It might seem a little cumbersome at first, but with practice we can invoke those four qualities swiftly and quietly and be on our way again.

CONCLUSION

The Metta Bhavana rightly has a reputation for making possible the radical transformation of our emotions, and our emotions are largely what form our view of ourselves and the world. So through this practice we can transform our basic experience of life. We can live in a new world of expansiveness, kindness, and love. Inasmuch as we can develop metta without regard to our own benefit, we can expand our hearts to include consideration for other beings in a way that softens and opens the barriers between ourselves and others. With time and practice this will undermine the conviction of our separate and precious selfhood, and we can come to experience things more as the Buddha did, things as they really are, inter-connected and interdependent. Through the practice of the Metta Bhavana and its effect on our lives we might even see a clearer way to social and political peace. To do so we need to fully understand and realize the truth of the uncompromising words of the Buddha, taken from the first section of the *Dhammapada*, the best-known of all Buddhist texts:

> Not by hatred are hatreds ever pacified here (in the world). They are pacified by love. This is the eternal law.*

* *Dhammapada* 5, trans. Sangharakshita (unpublished).

Putting Oneself First

by Abhaya

In his commentary on the Metta Bhavana meditation practice, Buddhaghosa tells the story of four monks who are walking through a forest one day when they are captured by bandits. 'Give us a monk!' demands the bandit chief, who wants a sacrificial victim. Which one is the senior monk to choose? Offering himself in preference to the others, Buddhaghosa insists, is no way out of the dilemma. He uses the story to illustrate his point that the meditator should develop loving kindness just as much for himself as for the other three people he has chosen: friend, neutral person, and enemy. There should not be the slightest hint of a bias in favour of one rather than the others. If the monk thinks 'Let them take me but not these three,' he has not, as Buddhaghosa puts it, broken down the barriers; he lacks metta towards his own self.

The development of metta towards oneself is the first stage of the practice as it has come down to us through the centuries. When I sit down to meditate I do not start by developing metta for my friend or the person next door. I start with myself. This is not because one's own self is any more important than others. It points rather to something unfortunately common amongst us — the tendency to undervalue ourselves. Working against this, one puts oneself in the first stage and loving kindness for oneself becomes the foundation of genuine altruism. Metta for others flows out of self-metta. The aspiring bodhisattva, who would devote all his energies to the growth and development of others, can do so only if he first feels well disposed towards himself.

This shining of the light of good will on oneself is something that many find curious, if not difficult, when they first try the meditation. It goes against the bias of entrenched habit. I know from my own experience of introducing the meditation to others that the very idea of developing loving kindness towards oneself can come as a shock to the aspiring meditator. I have seen eyebrows raised at the very suggestion that one could possibly begin a serious religious practice by putting oneself before others. Surely it is a rather selfish thing to do! The Buddha himself challenges such doubts when he says, in the *Udana (5.1)*:

I visited all quarters with my mind,
Nor found I any dearer than myself,
Self is likewise to every other dear;
Who loves himself will never harm another.

It need hardly be said that what the Buddha means here is a very healthy self-regard, a caring for oneself as no less or no more dear than any other living being. It is in no sense a putting of oneself first at the expense of others, and has nothing at all to do with what is commonly understood as selfishness or narcissistic obsession.

It is wonderful to hear the Enlightened One encouraging us so unequivocally to love ourselves. What better spur to get on with the Metta Bhavana? Yet, when one actually sits down to meditate, this first stage can be daunting. Faced at the start with either the opposite of love for self or, apparently, nothing at all, even seasoned meditators are tempted to do the Mindfulness of Breathing practice instead! Challenging though it is to keep the mind on the breathing, one's breath seems less elusive than an emotion.

For that is what metta essentially is: an emotion. It is not 'thinking about myself' as beginners sometimes put it. Metta is a very potent positive emotion, 'mightily powerful' as Buddhaghosa calls it. It is so powerful that the words at our disposal to translate it, such as 'friendliness', 'loving kindness', and 'good will' sound weak and inadequate, although these may well be the qualities we contact in ourselves when first doing the practice. Yet at its most powerful, metta is the first of the sublime abodes; if one succeeds in contacting and developing metta, one 'abides' or dwells in a god-like condition, a sublime state of being. Metta is frequently evoked in poetic terms. It is 'incandescent'; it 'shines, it glows, it blazes forth'. But here I sit, poised on my cushion, ready to begin, yet feeling far from sublime! How can I develop such an exalted state of being if I lack even a spark of it for myself? And if there is a spark, how do I fan the flame?

The traditional method is gently to coax oneself into a feeling of well-being by repeating the wish: 'May I be well; may I be happy.' At first this might feel a bit wooden, and if there is no immediate response it is easy to slide into mechanical repetition. We have to give ourselves the chance to mean it by pausing and letting the aspiration really sink in. As we blow on the ashes, sooner or later the hard block of resistance starts to melt and our emotional state becomes more fluid.

Another method of contacting good will towards oneself is through association. By recalling an occasion in the past, either recent or distant, when we were very well and happy, completely at ease with ourselves, we can re-contact the feeling itself in the present moment. Taking care not to be waylaid into discursive thinking about the past, we simply dwell on the memory and focus on the feeling we then had.

Once we have succeeded in reconnecting with the feeling we have a real foundation for wishing ourselves well. We can then revert to the traditional method. If that doesn't seem to work, we can experiment. Some people prefer a more visual approach. One might, for instance, visualize a bright ball of light at the heart centre that glows and steadily expands, or a deep red lotus flower radiating its warmth in all directions.

We should always be able to find at least one positive element in our mental state when we sit down to meditate. It could be something very down-to-earth such as a feeling of satisfaction that a job has gone well, or the physical sensation of sitting in a relaxed and easy posture. It may not be immediately evident because when we first sit to meditate, we are often, for one reason or another, a bit out of touch with ourselves. It is worth spending the first few minutes contacting that positive factor; we can then use it as a basis from which to develop self-metta.

It has to be admitted that sometimes whatever we try does not seem to work, and we feel stuck with either the negative emotion we started with or a total lack of feeling. It is important to acknowledge this. Perhaps in such a situation the best one can do is just to sit quietly for a while and not pretend that things are otherwise. It may be that this relaxing of all effort is just what was needed and our mental state begins to change for the better.

Metta is the antidote to the poison of hatred or ill will. We may not go so far as to hate ourselves; our difficulty could be a lack of self-confidence. Whatever we call it, its roots go deep, and the process of transformation is not going to be experienced in a single session. The effects of working in the first stage are cumulative. We may not notice any dramatic change during the fifty minutes we spend meditating, but most people feel some of the benefits of regular practice within a relatively short time, certainly within weeks, if not days.

Sometimes the effects are much more immediate. In a matter of minutes we can move out of the tight hole we have dug for ourselves of either dullness or resentment, into a bright space of expansive good will. As we begin, in the first stage of our Metta Bhavana practice, to break up the hard crust of our negative self-view, we gain access to deep reserves of positive emotion.

In the process, what was at first just an intellectual understanding gradually becomes a matter of living experience. We see that the source of our own well-being is deep within us, an inexhaustible treasure-store to which the first stage of the Metta Bhavana is a key. It comes as a profound relief to realize that true contentment is not something that anyone else can take away, that we do not depend for our well-being and contentment on anyone or anything outside ourselves.

When we have our first glimpse, even our first dip in the ocean, of metta, the cause of all malice and ill will is removed, or at least temporarily suspended. We see that the refreshing waters are for others just as much as for ourselves, and we begin genuinely to want to draw others in. In this way the metta we have generated begins, quite spontaneously, to overflow into the second stage of the practice.

Opening the Floodgates

by Vidyasri

In the second stage of the Metta Bhavana practice we contact and develop feelings of loving kindness towards a good friend. Traditional guidelines suggest that we choose someone who is alive, someone roughly the same age as ourselves, and someone to whom we are not sexually attracted. These guidelines help us contact a relatively straightforward flow of emotion in the practice. It is not that other types of relationships are wrong in any way, but it is only realistic to acknowledge that our feelings and responses within them may be more complex, as they often involve many of our more personal needs and desires.

Seeing our friend before us in our mind's eye as clearly and vividly as possible, we *feel* their presence and become aware of our response to them. The idea is not in any way to force or impose friendly, 'mettaful' feelings on ourselves, or merely to 'think' them – but to allow our *actual* positive feelings for that person to surface. At first, these feelings may not be very strong – they may be little more than a trickle of warmth and well-wishing. But we focus on that trickle, stay with it, allow ourselves to feel it more strongly, trying to follow it back towards its source.

Our minds are often too scattered to rest on anything for very long. This makes it impossible for us to contact the full extent of our feelings in response to things and people. But in the meditation we give ourselves the time and space to contact at least a stirring of the warmth that we feel. We gently focus and dwell on that feeling, allowing ourselves to feel it more strongly and more fully, allowing it to expand and deepen.

We can help this process get started by using memories. For instance, we can recollect a time when we were with our friend and felt full of appreciation and good feelings for them; a time when they were really happy, fulfilled, and expansive. Or we can imagine them in a situation in which we know they would feel happy and free from suffering. Perhaps we see them sitting on an expanse of golden sand, with a sparkling blue sea lapping peacefully along the shore and a warm golden sun shining down on them, or in a lush garden surrounded by trees, flowers, and fragrant scents. From these memories we can go on to build genuine feelings of metta for our friend, wishing them well and happy whatever their state of mind or current situation.

It is best to keep any such imaginative fantasies fairly simple so that we don't find ourselves wandering off and getting lost in them. The important thing is that we should contact genuine feelings of well-wishing and allow them to deepen and expand until, ideally, our whole consciousness and being become saturated with the strength of our metta.

If we bear this central point in mind we can be spontaneous and imaginative in our approach. Some people find that evoking colours can help focus and deepen their positive feelings. I often find myself giving my friend a beautiful deep-red rose which exudes a fragrance that fills their whole being, permeating them with contentment and happiness. As in the other stages, words or phrases can be a good aid to focusing and cultivating feelings – so long as the words are *felt* and not just repeated mechanically: 'May you be truly well and happy; may you be free from suffering; may you experience happiness and its causes.'

Sometimes we simply need to remain aware of our friend clearly 'before us', staying with the positive feelings of well-wishing, appreciation, and encouragement that arise within us in response to them. Perhaps, as we become more familiar and experienced with the practice, this stage can be as simple as that. We just allow ourselves to see more and more deeply and fully into our friend, experiencing the warmth, care, openness, and love that are part of this 'seeing'.

In this stage of the practice we are trying to contact and involve whatever positive emotions and energies are already present within us. We are 'opening the floodgates' to our free-flowing positive emotion, *allowing* it to flow by bringing it more into consciousness, and then developing it further. For many people this is the easiest stage in the practice, for the door to our metta is already partially open. (We can then carry these feelings into the other stages of the practice, and eventually feel as strongly towards others as we do towards our good friend.) We do not focus on what our friend can do or give to *us*, but on what we feel for *them*, in themselves.

Besides being an important stage in the process of contacting and generating an attitude of metta towards all sentient beings, this stage helps us to acknowledge more fully the positive feelings we *do* have for our friends and to strengthen them, thus helping us to develop our friendships. In my own practice I have sometimes suddenly felt the full force of my positive feelings for someone – and have thus realized that I am usually conscious of only a fraction of their force. It is almost as if we fear the strength of our feelings. But in this second stage we have the opportunity to expand the boundaries of our heart, to experience the full force of our positive emotion.

Of course it is not enough just to try to develop an *attitude* of metta towards all sentient beings. We also need to *act*, to live this metta out in the course of our interactions and relationships. It is only then that we will really begin to transform ourselves and the world. And although we can interact in a friendly way with a limitless number of people, it is only with a few that we can develop a close friendship and share ourselves and our lives in a more detailed and intimate way.

Sadly, it seems that fulfilling friendships play little or no part in many people's lives in the West today, perhaps less than in any previous generation. Psychologists and counsellors are discovering that we need friendships to ensure a healthy mental state. Buddhism would go further than this. According to Buddhism, while friendships are certainly necessary for our general health and happiness, they are, just as much as our meditation practice, a means of making progress in our spiritual development.

So why do we struggle so with our friendships – to maintain them over long periods of time, or even to create them in the first place? The truth is that many of us find it painfully difficult to trust other people, and hence, though longing for intimacy, we fear the exposure that intimacy involves. Thus we withhold our commitment to the task of building up a friendship. So often, too, we have a vested interest in who and what someone is and does; we desire them to be what *we* want them to be, to compensate for, or to complement, what we are. Or we identify with and relate through roles – at work, at home, even at the Buddhist centre. At times we feel superior, at others inferior. In short, we do not feel secure, whole, or content in ourselves. Thus our security and even our identity can become entangled with and dependent upon those around us, coloured by our deep biases of craving or aversion.

But also present in our relationships with other people there is usually a thread of genuine care, even love, which may be more or less present at different times. It is this element that is the real basis of a friendship; this is the soil from which a friendship can grow and flourish. The more we can develop and cultivate this field of metta within us, both inside and outside our practice of the Metta Bhavana, the more happiness and benefit both we and our friend will experience in each other's company. Letting go of our expectations we can learn to feel for and empathize with our friend in their own right. We can gradually come to see them more and more as they truly are. Thus, as the intensity of our metta develops, so too does our awareness and understanding of our friend.

Through developing metta we can build up our capacity to trust – to trust both ourselves and others. It is, of course, much easier to develop trust in someone if they too are consciously attempting to relate on a basis of metta. With this 'security' we can gradually begin to trust each other's overall intentions, even if we still act selfishly at times. Gradually, a sense of commitment and fidelity will arise which is integral to the health – or continuation – of any friendship. Friendships often suffer from a discontinuity not only of physical contact but also of awareness: out of sight, our friend can be 'out of mind'. This will result in a rather superficial or fragmented relationship. Regularly focusing on our friends during the Metta Bhavana practice will help us maintain a continuity of awareness of our friend in our heart and consciousness, keeping the channels of communication alive and open through the days, weeks, and even years when we are physically apart.

These days, many people suffer from intense loneliness. They feel a sense of isolation and separateness from the millions of people all around them. To have even a few good close friends can make a great difference. To connect deeply and openly with a few other people will help us to feel connected to the whole world, for it is our own minds and hearts that are shut off. As we begin to love and care for another as for ourself, the sharp distinction between our 'self' and the 'other' will gradually soften, leaving us to feel the fundamental non-difference between ourselves and our friend – which eventually we can experience between ourselves and all other beings.

Breaking Down the Barriers of Prejudice

by Dhammadinna

Introducing a 'neutral' person into the Metta Bhavana brings about a crucial transition in the practice. It marks the beginning of the development of loving kindness in its fullest sense.

Metta, in contrast with *pema* or 'attachment', has an unconditional, universal dimension to it. Most of us can care for ourselves and for our close family and friends. We may therefore find it comparatively easy to cultivate feelings of warmth and friendliness in the first and second stages of the practice. However, to develop feelings of genuine well-wishing towards a neutral person is obviously much more of a challenge. Here, we are attempting to move from a lack of interest at best — and boredom at worst — to warmth and concern for people we do not know and in whom we have no vested interest.

During this stage of the practice we may lose our momentum because we have such weak feelings as our basis. We have less emotional intensity to draw upon and are therefore more prone to distraction. As a result the mental image of the neutral person may soon fade.

We can work consciously with this tendency, but we also need to stimulate our interest, not only in the neutral person, but in the significance of this stage as a whole. We can do this by reflecting on some of the underlying attitudes that are challenged in this stage. Why are we uncaring towards people just because we do not know them? Perhaps we take it for granted that there is no need really to care about such people. But, on reflection, we may turn the question around and wonder why *not* care for those we do not know?

Surely, we are only emotionally neutral towards some people because we prefer to remain within fixed boundaries, within the known and the safe. To be unable to extend metta towards those we do not know implies not only a lack of interest, but also a failure to understand our connectedness with other people. It may also suggest that we are lazy and complacent about our emotional involvements.

However, before returning to ways of working with these underlying attitudes, we need to explore more fully who exactly these 'neutral' people are.

A neutral person can be anyone we do not know or have any feeling for. These are people we pass in the street or while travelling out and about. There are some who cross our path more regularly; we may see them at work, or travel with them regularly, without developing any particular feelings towards them. They may be local shopkeepers, the postman, or our neighbours. Then again, we may feel neutral towards people we meet very often.

We may even find ourselves living and working with people towards whom, we must admit, we feel more or less neutral.

In our crowded society we are regularly brought into close proximity with strangers. In such circumstances our attitude can be to experience others as, at least, something of a nuisance. Paradoxically, it is often easier to feel emotionally caring towards the strangers we see – especially if they are suffering – on our televisions or in our newspapers than towards those we encounter every day. These feelings may be genuinely compassionate or they may provide an outlet for an emotion that is closer to sentimentality or pity. Again, we need to distinguish metta or loving kindness from compassion. Compassion is a response to the suffering of others, and grows from a basis of loving kindness.

Feeling metta towards the many neutral strangers in our lives involves systematically cultivating, on a day to day level, feelings of friendliness towards people we come into actual contact with. In the practice itself we therefore choose someone who crosses our path regularly but towards whom we have no particularly strong feelings. It definitely helps if we can picture that person in our mind's eye and get at least a sense of them.

If we reflect upon our relationship with such a neutral person, we may come to see that our lack of feeling is actually a reflection of our own emotional limitations and prejudices rather than a meaningful statement about their character. Only our own emotional laziness prevents us from fully experiencing and engaging with them. If we explore these limitations we may find them expressed in such thoughts as 'Why should I like this person? They have done nothing for me! There is nothing in it for me!' Thus we discover that – on a gross or subtle level – we are really only interested in being involved with people who are going to give us something in return. This is why cultivating metta towards a neutral person works against selfishness and craving and begins to open our hearts towards others simply in response to who they are.

These reflections on our basic attitudes and limitations will involve thinking quite deeply about the nature of metta and our purpose in engaging in the practice as a whole. Although metta may sometimes flow quite easily, and we may have a pleasant feeling within the practice itself, the pleasant feelings are not the aim of the practice. In the longer term we are working towards transforming our entire emotional nature, from one based on the giving of conditional love to one rooted in selfless love.

The expression of loving kindness is an aspect of the emotional nature of what we call the 'true individual'. A true individual can be defined as one who has emerged from the 'group', in that they think and feel for themselves and accept full responsibility for their own life and future.* A true individual cares for others on the basis of a perceived common humanity. It is through the develop-

*For a fuller explanation, see Sangharakshita, *New Currents in Western Buddhism*, Windhorse 1990, pp.20–33.

ment of metta that we can emancipate ourselves from the group, group conditioning, and group identification. Then the stranger becomes our brother or sister; the neutral person becomes our friend. We would be prepared to stand by them even if everyone else we know retreated behind the barriers of kith and kin, nation and race. Perhaps we can now begin to see the significance of this stage of the practice. Such reflections may even give us a glimpse of insight, a realization, however faint, that all life is interconnected, and that the subject–object, self–other dichotomy can be transcended.

Of course, we also need to find ways of working in the practice itself. We have seen that we can easily lose our momentum and fall prey to distraction during this stage. To begin with, then, it will help us if we remember in detail the steps leading towards the cultivation of metta in any stage. First of all we need to be in touch with positive feelings towards and within ourselves. Then we can introduce a mental impression of the neutral person. Next we acknowledge our present experience of them. We may discover, for example – since we are rarely absolutely neutral about anything – whether we tend towards very weak attraction or repulsion. Then we begin to cultivate positive feelings towards that person, and allow those feelings to develop. If we become distracted at any point we need to return to the first step, becoming aware of ourselves and then recontacting the image and cultivating metta for the neutral person.

Because we set out with little interest in the neutral person, we must find ways to engage our interest and emotionality. So we can perhaps reflect that this person is another human being with joys and sorrows of their own. We may find our emotions are more stimulated if we give our imagination free rein. Perhaps we can imagine the person — who for us is just a face on the train — at home, with their family, actually living out their life. We can allow this imaginative fantasy to unfold and take on a life of its own, all the time keeping the mental image of the person in mind and staying aware of our emotional response to them.

Because of our disinterest we will probably see the person rather one-dimensionally, more like a cardboard cut-out than a real person. Our imagination allows us to flesh them out, creating more dimensions to their life that we can engage with emotionally. Imagination itself is a creative, non-utilitarian faculty; through it we can change an essentially utilitarian perception of, say, the local shop assistant who is fulfilling a role for us, so that they become alive and real for us and we can then actively wish them well.

According to Gampopa's *Jewel Ornament of Liberation*, another means of developing metta is the contemplation of benefits received. This suggests that metta grows from a feeling of genuine gratitude. If our relationship with the neutral person *is* essentially utilitarian — perhaps they do sell us vegetables every day — we can reflect that without vegetables we would not be able to sustain life.

Thus we can feel gratitude towards that person, as well as towards that chain of people who help put food on our plates. Such reflections may help us cultivate feelings of metta at the beginning of the practice or in the third stage itself.

Obviously we can also cultivate loving kindness, awareness of others, and open communication, in everyday life. We can *choose* to interact more positively with those we meet. Even taking and showing a little friendly interest in the people we meet in passing can make a difference to our lives – and theirs. Rather than being bored on the train or the bus we can at least take note of our fellow travellers and be open to them as other human beings. We can develop an imaginative involvement in their lives which opens the channels for feelings of warmth and well-wishing to flow. We may also find that the people we put into our neutral stage become more interested in us! Deeper contact, even friendship, may develop just by virtue of our having become more emotionally open to someone during the metta practice.

The development of metta towards people we feel neutral towards can have subtle and far-reaching effects. We may find our life and communication in general more emotionally satisfying. We may make new friends. We are also tackling some deep underlying attitudes of selfishness and self-concern that block our growth and development. Put more positively, by working in this stage we begin to experience the dissolution of the barriers we erect between ourselves and others. Our hearts open and we begin to experience that free flow of unconditional love that enables us to feel happy in ourselves and responsive to all those we meet.

The Alchemy of Emotion

by Chris Pauling

The fourth stage of the Metta Bhavana could be likened
to an alchemical experiment: two incompatible
substances are forced together in a closed vessel until,
eventually, they unite to form a new compound, brighter
and more precious than either. One of the ingredients –
already bright and precious in its own right, but perhaps
still soft and fragile – is the metta we have built up in the
earlier stages of the practice. The other – dark, explosive,
and as hostile to the first as hot oil is to water – is our
anger or ill will. The closed vessel is our heart.

For the reaction to work we must start with the right
ingredients. We need a strong current of metta carried
over from the first three stages. We also need a genuine
source of ill will – so we should be honest, and choose
somebody we have real feelings towards. But at the same
time we must beware: anger is *very* explosive. If we choose
someone we are still furious with, our ill will may
overwhelm us – the vessel may be blown to pieces. A
sense of balance is needed.

We also need to supply the right conditions – we need to keep the ingredients together under pressure within our awareness. But keeping our attention on two quite different emotions can be difficult. Again it requires balance.

Sometimes the balance slips too far one way – our metta deserts us, and we become lost in ill will. When this happens the best thing is to forget the 'enemy' for a while and go back to an earlier stage of the practice to recontact the warmth in our heart.

Sometimes the balance slips in the other direction – we gloss over our real feelings for our 'enemy', losing ourselves in a hazy, impersonal glow of pleasant emotions. Then we need to come down from our cloud and bring the real-life person back to mind as clearly as possible.

Metta tends to transform the baser elements of our nature into gold. If we succeed in keeping our balance, this transmuting effect on its own may be enough to purify our resentments and refine the energy locked up in our anger. But often this is not enough, and we need to supply a catalyst to help the reaction along – everyone needs to develop their own techniques.

Personally, I find it particularly helpful to use my imagination to give myself more empathy with my 'enemy's' point of view. I call to mind the circumstances of their life, and the sorrows and suffering that these cause. I try to imagine myself inhabiting their body, and looking out from behind their eyes. I strive to make these imaginings as concrete as possible, by conjuring up real situations in all the detail I can muster: I imagine myself getting up in the morning as that other person, and seeing the sights they see; I imagine the situations they experience; I recreate past occasions when the two of us have been together, but as my 'enemy' must have perceived them.

By using the imagination in this way we can begin to get a tiny glimpse of what it means to transcend our limited, personal point of view. This glimpse is dim and fleeting, but still powerful — under its influence our ill will becomes lighter, more transparent, and less hostile to the metta in our heart. Then gradually, miraculously, the two begin to fuse, and in a flash the magic happens. When the smoke clears the dross has disappeared, and we are left with a jewel. Our love has combined with the energy of our anger. Our good will has been tempered by the realities of the world, and is fit to survive the rough and tumble of life in the human realm.

So far, I have been talking about the fourth stage at its best and most potent, but it would be wrong to expect it to be like this always, or even often. For those of us who are habitually troubled by ill will this part of the practice helps us to chip gradually away at our emotional habits. Many of the benefits come in unglamorous ways: from aspects of the practice that at first sight seem unimportant; from making the effort and taking the time to think about our feelings and relationships; and from trying to take the lessons we learn out into our everyday life.

Before we even start the meditation we have to choose our 'enemy' – and this in itself is a useful part of the practice. Many newcomers to the Metta Bhavana find it difficult to think of anyone to cast in this role. By contrast, most people who have practised for some time have many more candidates jostling for a place in their fourth stage than they had when they started.

These meditators have not become worse-tempered; they have become more aware of their unspoken antagonism, anger, and resentment. This is partly because the regular practice of calling an 'enemy' to mind has helped them confront their comfortable assumptions about themselves and their relationships, and so bring their real feelings up into the light.

Having chosen someone to work with in our meditation, it is worth giving some thought to the nature of our feelings for this person, and to the reasons we feel as we do. At least three different types of 'enemy' make an appearance in our fourth stage.

Some are people who just seem to irritate us. They may not do or say anything against us, but their very presence seems to jar. In my own experience, whenever I have taken this sort of dislike to someone it has been because they have characteristics that I share, but have not acknowledged in myself. This is a common experience, and for this reason it is usually productive to consider honestly what it is about the other person that we dislike, and whether we might not sometimes behave – or want to behave – in exactly the same way. We can learn a lot about ourselves from thinking about our enemies.

The second class of people who belong in our fourth stage are those for whom we harbour lingering anger or resentment because of unfinished emotional business. These are often people we are *supposed* to be close to – we must beware that we don't dismiss people from consideration as 'enemies' because we *should* like, respect, or even love them. Our closest relationships are often the most fertile breeding grounds for ill will.

In such cases it is not enough to feel a few moments of warmth towards the person concerned, and leave it at that. This stage of the practice should be just one aspect of a constant process of uncovering and healing the rifts that cut us off from other people. The few minutes we spend each day in meditation can alert us to the fact that a rift exists, and give us the good will and positivity to do something creative to mend it. But the hard work starts when we leave our cushion.

This work consists in healing the wounds in our friendships by means of honest communication. What usually stands in the way of this healing is fear, masquerading as reserve and politeness. Overcoming our fear takes courage – including the courage needed to express our anger as skilfully as we know how. In the words of William Blake:

I was angry with my friend:
I told my wrath, my wrath did end.

I was angry with my foe:
I told it not, my wrath did grow.

One of the effects of this stage of the practice should be that we never allow our wrath to grow.

The last and least common inhabitants of our fourth stage are our true enemies: people who oppose our goals, or whose goals we oppose: people with whom we are in genuine conflict. Even when we have sorted out all our psychological quirks and communication difficulties, when we have extended the hand of friendship to all who will take it, a hard core of such antagonists may remain. Conflict is a feature of life – or at least of action – in the human realm.

Our usual response to conflict is either to avoid it – often by having no real goals of our own, but conforming to others' wishes – or to react with aggression. As Buddhists we should be seeking a more creative approach, one that allows us to act vigorously in the world, but with metta for those who oppose us.

To do this we need to rise above our unskilful emotional reactions, whilst still having access to the energy of our fear and aggression. This – at first sight impossible – refinement of our energies is the transmutation for which we are striving in the fourth stage of the meditation at its best. When we have achieved this we can bring the full power of our being to the fifth stage, and begin to genuinely feel – and act from – metta for all beings.

Opening our Hearts to the World

by Lokamitra

The first four stages of the Metta Bhavana are really a preparation for the fifth and final stage when feelings of metta are radiated throughout the world. Metta is traditionally known as one of the *appamanna* states, meaning 'boundless', 'limitless'. In this connection Sangharakshita has made the point that the tendency of positive emotions is to expand, whereas that of negative emotions is to contract, to become more limited. So in this stage we try to develop metta in such a way as to include all human beings, all life. We aim at a state of mind that spontaneously responds with metta when meeting another person, whether in our imagination or in the flesh.

We begin by bringing together the four people we have been concentrating on in the previous stages, and directing our metta to all of them at the same time. The emotional state we are trying to develop is one in which we feel a strong but absolutely equal love for all four. Were the bandits conjured up by Buddhaghosa in the *Vissuddhimagga* (see p.24) to ask us for the life of one of them we would be unable to choose – not because of any *lack* of feeling, but because of the *fullness* of our feeling for each. Clearly this emotion we are trying to develop is much more than just friendliness – it is a very strong, warm, caring, and cherishing love.

This is really the culmination of the whole Metta Bhavana practice, and is rather like bringing our positive feelings towards the different individuals together in a crucible. With the heat of our metta we try to melt down any differences in our feelings towards each of the individuals, until our metta is flowing freely and without barriers between all four persons. The more successful we are here the more easily will we be able to radiate that heat steadily throughout the world.

We now proceed to do this by bringing to mind all the people we are meditating with, and then expand the feelings of metta out to the street, the locality, the town, the region, the country, the continent, and all the different continents of the world. Alternatively we can take the different directions of space one at a time, or we can just radiate out in ever-increasing circles from where we are. But however we approach this stage of the practice we are trying (and if we have succeeded in bringing the four people together it will not be so much a question of trying as of a spontaneous flow of energy) to pervade and suffuse all beings everywhere, without exception, with feelings of metta. The words of the Buddha in the *Karaniya Metta Sutta* make this very clear:

May all be happy and feel secure. May all beings become happy in their heart of hearts!

And think of every living thing without exception: the weak and the strong, from the smallest to the largest, whether you can see them or not, living nearby or far away, beings living now or yet to arise – may all beings become happy in their heart of hearts!

May no one deceive or look down on anyone anywhere, for any reason. Whether through feeling angry or through reacting to someone else, may no one want another to suffer.

As strongly as a mother, perhaps risking her life, cherishes her child, her only child, develop an unlimited heart for all beings.

Develop an unlimited heart of friendliness for the entire universe, sending metta above, below, and all around, beyond all narrowness, beyond all rivalry, beyond all hatred.

One is not of course bound to the words of the Buddha. Doing the practice regularly one will probably create images and phrases of one's own that help in developing these supreme emotions. I often find it helpful to conclude the practice by thinking of all men, all women, all young, all old, all middle-aged, all at present being born, all at present dying, all rich, all poor, all happy, all sad, all free, all oppressed, all ill, all healthy, people of all religions, all races, and all nationalities.

As we travel around the world in our imagination we may find it hard to reconcile the different experiences of people – some are very happy and materially satisfied, while others are suffering through poverty, violence, war, famine, and exploitation. Doing the practice where I live, in Poona, one cannot ignore the poverty and the violence, not only on one's very doorstep and throughout India, but in all the surrounding countries – Tibet, Sri Lanka, Pakistan, Burma, Afghanistan, Kuwait, Iraq, and so on. At times it's very hard not to feel sad and depressed, so much so that our feelings of metta towards ourselves are affected. We can end up in a state of despair. We get stuck. We can no longer develop skilful mental states towards ourselves or other people. At the same time, when we encounter people who are happy we may find it hard not to respond to them with resentment when we see so much suffering.

This could mean that we have been putting too much emphasis on the phrases we repeat, and not enough on opening our hearts to ourselves and the three others. We may not have acknowledged our own unhappiness or negativity when we started the practice. The words go round in our head without connecting up with our hearts, and we cannot identify with others in any heartfelt way. The metta we develop will therefore only be an idea of metta, not a feeling, and therefore we cannot respond easily to the differences we find among people.

Moving from head to heart is difficult for a lot of people at first. I found this myself, and as such I could not easily feel for other human beings, let alone myself. I found reflecting on nature useful. I remember being confronted by this difficulty when trying to do a lot of

Metta Bhavana practice on my first solitary retreat. I was in a tent at the southern tip of the English Cotswolds, surrounded by trees. Eating outside, I spent a lot of time looking at the trees. Each tree was quite different in shape. Some were tall, some were short, some were wide spread and some slender. Each had different branches broken. There was a uniqueness about each tree, and yet in this uniqueness there was a definite unity. I found it very easy to translate the trees into human beings, and when I did that I found that feelings of metta arose spontaneously. I could identify quite easily with others. We are all born, we are all going to die. We all experience varying degrees of happiness and suffering. And yet we are all unique. There has never been anyone the same as us and there never will be. This imaginative identification with others is really the key to the success of the Metta Bhavana practice.

Metta adapts to different people in different situations. It expands to include mudita (sympathetic joy) and karuna (compassion). Instead of being resentful or jealous about the happiness of others, with a strong basis of metta we learn to respond with joy. And instead of getting over-emotional and being brought down by the suffering of others we can learn to respond with a soft smile on our faces, more able to understand. In this way the Metta Bhavana helps us to face the difficulties in life that inevitably come our way, whether they appear to come from within us or from outside. Instead of being discouraged and held back by them, we learn to approach them creatively, allowing them less and less to ensnare our positive emotions. Indeed, we gradually learn to regard them as opportunities to cultivate and test these positive states of mind.

When the practice goes very well, metta, extended to all, and unassailable by any negative thoughts, becomes equanimity (*upekkha*). There is no reactivity in one's mind, but this is far from indifference. One's positivity towards others is not compromised, no matter how negative or unskilful they may be. Such experiences may be some way off for most of us but, even so, if one applies oneself to this practice, especially on retreat, one can soon get a glimpse of this state.

The sitting meditation is only the beginning of the Metta Bhavana practice. How often do we come out of a good session of Metta Bhavana and immediately get annoyed at some petty occurrence? This is a rather salutary reminder that unless we consciously work to take what we have learned from meditation out into the rest of our lives, our behaviour will still be at the mercy of our old and deep reactive patterns. This means acknowledging, often again and again, that our emotions are far from what we would like them to be. But, painful though it may be, this is the basis for the process of emotional transformation. Slowly, maybe, but steadily, we will be able to take the Metta Bhavana out of the meditation room and find our hearts opening to the world.

Life, Love, Power, and Violence

by Nagabodhi

> Even if bandits were to sever you savagely with a
> two-handled saw, he who gave rise to a mind of hate
> towards them would not be carrying out my teaching.*

It must be more than twenty years since I first read those
words, yet I can still recall the enormous force with
which their unambiguous conviction hit me. The senti-
ment behind them was hardly new; I had grown up in a
culture where the idea of 'loving your enemy' was a stock
platitude. But there was, and is, something about the
uncomfortably graphic detail with which the Buddha
chose to express himself that demands an entirely new
kind of attention, reflection, and response. Did the
Buddha really mean what he was saying, or was he
exaggerating a little to make a point – the nice familiar
one about loving your enemies, and perhaps occasionally
'turning the other cheek'?

There seem to be two aspects to the problem. To put
up with enemies, and even to meet their assaults with an

* *Kakacupama Sutta*, Majjhima-Nikaya 21, trans. Bhikkhu Nanamoli and
Bhikkhu Bodhi.

attempt at positive thought, feeling, and action, is one thing. But to be able, in the heat – even the agony – of the moment, to feel nothing but love for them demands a state of such profound and complete *preparedness* that the mind staggers at the prospect of the work involved. Then there are the enemies themselves. Like countless people with whom I've spoken after their first attempt at the Metta Bhavana, I have sometimes wondered whether there might not be a few 'enemies' who deserve to languish for ever in that category: 'Should one really try to develop metta for someone like *Hitler*?' 'What about oppressive governments?'

Regarding the first problem, there seems to be no getting away from the fact that the Buddha really did mean what he was saying. Had he not confronted Devadatta, Angulimala, and other villains with tolerance and love? Had he not offered the full benefit of his teaching to Ajatasattu, a man who had taken the throne by killing his own father?

The preparatory work involved was of course nothing less than the spiritual path he had discovered and shared. In offering this precept, therefore, he was not inviting us to pretend that we feel love when we do not, or to try to ignore the malice in the world – and our suffering – by an effort of sheer will; a two-handed saw, I fear, would cut its way as efficiently through to the truth of one's fundamental emotional state as it would to one's bones! But this is the very point of the Buddha's message. In choosing such a powerful image he was not only guarding against the possibility of a purely sentimental or superficial response: he was implicitly assuring us that a point is reached, somewhere along the spiritual path, where our identification with, and experience of, the universe, others, our bodies, and even our 'selves', will be dramatically different. As the Mahayana scholar-poet, Shantideva, says when talking of self-sacrifice:

At the beginning, the Guide of the World encourages
The giving of such things as food.
Later, when accustomed to this,
One may progressively start to give away even one's flesh.

At such a time when my mind is developed
To the point of regarding my body like food,
Then what hardship would there be
When it came to giving away my flesh?*

Kshanti, 'patient forbearance', is to be *practised* at all times, right from the beginning of our spiritual career, but it will only be '*perfected*' when it is infused with the highest wisdom. And that wisdom is the fruit of all our practice. So practise we must.

The solution to this first problem naturally goes some way towards providing a solution to the second. When we no longer see things in a deluded, ego-centred way: when we see the universe and all it contains, including our bodies, moods, thoughts, feelings, and 'selves' – and

* *A Guide to the Bodhisattva's Way of Life* trans. Stephen Batchelor, Tibetan Library of Works and Archives, Dharamsala 1981, p.90.

those of others – as a dynamic interplay of ephemeral conditions, then, naturally enough, we will no longer see enemies as enemies in quite the way we do now. To come down to earth a little, we may see them as helpless beings trapped in webs of their own conditioning, their own delusions, their own impulses – perhaps even causing themselves far more suffering than they are capable of inflicting upon others. And our spontaneous response towards them can only be metta, in the form of compassion.

But, meanwhile ... while we do not yet see them in that way, and while their actions continue to cause very tangible suffering, what are we to make of them? And what are we to do? What *are* we to do about the Adolf Hitlers and the Saddam Husseins, or, for that matter, the noisy neighbour and the vindictive colleague?

If the emotional reflex of wisdom is a love born of selflessness, and its dynamic fruits are disinterested actions rooted in that love, then it is perhaps worth wondering what might be the emotional reflex, and what the fruits, of ignorance. The reflex, surely, is none other than the well-known triad of greed, hatred, and delusion born of self-centredness, while the dynamic fruits are ego-bolstering acts, rooted of course in greed, hatred, and delusion, but dependent on the *power* contained in those emotions, and in our bodies, for their accomplishment.

No matter how far we may be from Enlightenment, we would do well to try to see the difference between the exercise of love and of power, whether in others or in ourselves. Sangharakshita has spoken of a love *mode* and a power *mode*; in gaining some clarity over this distinction we can move towards a recipe for Buddhist action.

By and large, the world – both metaphorical and actual – is driven by power. To get what they want, and to avoid what they do not want, people use physical force, moral blackmail, manipulation gross and subtle, economic pressure, political platforms; they play seduction games, offer threats, make false promises, and so on. They deploy whatever power they have, either by exercising it or by withholding it. With such forces constantly at play, is it surprising that things sometimes get out of hand?

In such a world, a Buddhist has two major responsibilities. First, he or she must practise the Dharma in its fullness, so as to become, eventually, a beacon of wisdom and love in the midst of darkness. Second, by applying awareness and discrimination, every effort should be made to refrain from functioning in the power mode and to function instead in the love mode. This means, among other things, abandoning all forms of coercion for reasoned discussion and dialogue, abandoning manipulation for direct and truthful communication, abandoning resentment and grudges for honest self-examination, abandoning undermining gossip for constructive criticism, and – when appropriate – a wholehearted rejoicing in merits.

Actions issuing from the love mode are creative, energetic, and probably far more effective than most people realize. Arguably, there may be times, despite our best efforts, when the love mode does not seem to be getting through, and when an excursion into the power mode might seem likely to avert great harm; with the best will in the world, we cannot always answer for the intransigence of others. Again arguably, at such a time one might, reluctantly, resort to the power mode – but only as a *last* resort. In taking such a step we must above all be certain that we are not giving way to our own greed, hatred, or ignorance, and that we are using the power mode only in the *service* of the love mode. Thus, a caring parent might smack a child when reasoned discussion on the wisdom of pulling his sister's hair, or of placing his hand in the fire, has foundered. In a broader arena, it may be that the power mode can be most safely deployed by *withholding* one's power. Gandhi, actually a very shrewd and manipulative politician, made great, and often benign, use of non-violent, 'passive' resistance. This must be preferable to violence itself, but any resort to the power mode carries the seeds of danger, and should be forsaken as quickly as possible.

At the time of the Gulf War, I remember hearing many an ironical remark about the United Nations Organization's willingness to act on behalf of Kuwait while leaving Tibet to its fate. During a meeting with a body of academics and religious dignitaries in London, the Dalai Lama was provocatively asked whether he thought that a newly potent UNO might be good news for Tibet. His – initially reluctant – reply was a triumph of tact. The world, he said, is becoming increasingly interconnected, increasingly one system. Any organization, therefore, which encourages the development of unity and harmony in that one world can only be a good thing.

His audience murmured a knowing chuckle and I could not help wondering how many of them assumed that, behind his diplomatic restraint, the Dalai Lama was really hoping that the UNO *would* act, would resort to the power mode in relation to the China–Tibet issue. The situation is of course highly complex – as would be a war fought in the Himalayan heights rather than in a desert – and Tibet has no oil. (Indeed, its most precious asset, wisdom, has flowed around the world rather more freely *since* the Chinese invasion!)

Just or not, the liberation of Kuwait cost more than 100,000 lives. The liberation of Tibet, even were it militarily conceivable, could involve similar losses. The Dalai Lama is believed to be an emanation of Avalokiteshvara, the Bodhisattva of Supreme Compassion. Is that a price that he would be prepared to pay? What do you think? And what does your heart say?

The Karaniya Metta Sutta

If you know what is truly good for you and understand the possibility of reaching a state of perfect peace, then this is how you need to live.

Start as a capable person, who is upright (really upright), gently spoken, flexible, and not conceited.

Then become contented and happy, with few worries and an uncomplicated life.

Make sure your sense experience is calm and controlled, be duly respectful, and don't hanker after families or groups. And avoid doing anything unworthy, that wiser people would criticize.

(Then meditate like this:)
May all be happy and feel secure. May all beings become happy in their heart of hearts!

And think of every living thing without exception: the weak and the strong, from the smallest to the largest, whether you can see them or not, living

nearby or far away, beings living now or yet to arise —
may all beings become happy in their heart of hearts!

May no one deceive or look down on anyone
anywhere, for any reason. Whether through feeling
angry or through reacting to someone else, may no
one want another to suffer.

As strongly as a mother, perhaps risking her life,
cherishes her child, her only child, develop an
unlimited heart for all beings.

Develop an unlimited heart of friendliness for the
entire universe, sending metta above, below, and all
around, beyond all narrowness, beyond all rivalry,
beyond all hatred.

Whether you are staying in one place or travelling,
sitting down or in bed, in all your waking hours rest in
this mindfulness, which is known as like living in
heaven right here and now!

In this way, you will come to let go of views, be
spontaneously ethical, and have perfect Insight. And
leaving behind craving for sense pleasures, from the
rounds of rebirth you will finally be completely free!

Further Reading

Bodhipaksa, *Wildmind*, Windhorse, Birmingham 2003

Pema Chodron, *Awakening Loving Kindness*, Shambhala, Boston & London 1996

Jinananda, *Meditating*, Windhorse, Birmingham 2000

Ayya Khema, *Being Nobody, Going Nowhere*, Wisdom, Boston 1987

Paramananda, *Change Your Mind*, Windhorse, Birmingham 1996

Paramananda, *A Deeper Beauty*, Windhorse, Birmingham 2001

Sharon Salzberg, *Loving Kindness*, Shambhala, Boston & London 1995

Tejananda, *The Buddhist Path to Awakening*, Windhorse, Birmingham 1999

The windhorse symbolizes the energy of the Enlightened mind carrying the truth of the Buddha's teachings to all corners of the world. On its back the windhorse bears three jewels: a brilliant gold jewel represents the Buddha, the ideal of Enlightenment, a sparkling blue jewel represents the teachings of the Buddha, the Dharma, and a glowing red jewel, the community of the Buddha's enlightened followers, the Sangha. Windhorse Publications, through the medium of books, similarly takes these three jewels out to the world.

Windhorse Publications is a Buddhist publishing house, staffed by practising Buddhists. We place great emphasis on producing books of high quality, accessible and relevant to those interested in Buddhism at whatever level. Drawing on the whole range of the Buddhist tradition, Windhorse books include translations of traditional texts, commentaries, books that make links with Western culture and ways of life, biographies of Buddhists, and manuals on meditation.

For orders and catalogues log on to www.windhorsepublications.com or contact

WINDHORSE PUBLICATIONS	WINDHORSE BOOKS	WEATHERHILL INC
11 PARK ROAD	P O BOX 574	41 MONROE TURNPIKE
BIRMINGHAM	NEWTOWN	TRUMBULL
B13 8AB	NSW 2042	CT 06611
UK	AUSTRALIA	USA

Windhorse Publications is an arm of the Friends of the Western Buddhist Order, which has more than sixty centres on five continents. Through these centres, members of the Western Buddhist Order offer regular programmes of events for the general public and for more experienced students. These include meditation classes, public talks, study on Buddhist themes and texts, and 'bodywork' classes such as t'ai chi, yoga, and massage. The FWBO also runs several retreat centres and the Karuna Trust, a fund-raising charity that supports social welfare projects in the slums and villages of India.

Many FWBO centres have residential spiritual communities and ethical businesses associated with them. Arts activities are encouraged too, as is the development of strong bonds of friendship between people who share the same ideals. In this way the FWBO is developing a unique approach to Buddhism, not simply as a set of techniques, less still as an exotic cultural interest, but as a creatively directed way of life for people living in the modern world.

If you would like more information about the FWBO visit the website at www.fwbo.org or write to

LONDON BUDDHIST CENTRE
51 ROMAN ROAD
LONDON
E2 OHU
UK

ARYALOKA
HEARTWOOD CIRCLE
NEWMARKET
NH 03857
USA

ALSO FROM WINDHORSE

BODHIPAKSA

VEGETARIANISM

Part of a series on *Living a Buddhist Life*, this book explores connections between vegetarianism and the spiritual life.

As a trained vet, Bodhipaksa is well placed to reveal the suffering of animals in the farming industry, and as a practising Buddhist he can identify the ethical consequences of inflicting such suffering. Through the Buddhist teaching of interconnectedness he lays bare the effects our eating habits can have upon us, upon animals, and upon the environment.

He concludes that by becoming vegetarian we can affirm life in a very clear and immediate way, and so experience a greater sense of contentment, harmony, and happiness.

112 pages
ISBN 1 899579 15 x
£4.99/$7.95/€7.95

JINANANDA

MEDITATING

This is a guide to Buddhist meditation that is in sympathy with modern lifestyle. Accessible and thought-provoking, this books tells you what you need to know to get started with meditation, and keep going through the ups and downs of everyday life. Realistic, witty, and very inspiring.

136 pages
ISBN 1 899579 07 9
£4.99/$7.95/€7.95

SANGHADEVI

LIVING TOGETHER

Living Together explores the essential ingredients of community living, including friendliness, cooperation, meaningful communication, and mutual vision.

Drawing on her many years in Buddhist communities, Sanghadevi, a widely-respected Buddhist teacher, encourages those who aspire to this lifestyle to engage with the frequent challenges they will encounter and speaks from her experience of the joys of sharing.

112 pages
ISBN 1 899579 50 8
£4.99 / $7.95 / €7.95

SANGHARAKSHITA

RITUAL AND DEVOTION IN BUDDHISM: AN INTRODUCTION

For many people in the West, devotional practice is a confronting aspect of Buddhism which it is easier to ignore. Skilfully steering us through the difficulties we may encounter, Sangharakshita shows that ritual and devotion have a crucial role to play in our spiritual lives, because they speak the language of the heart. Leading us through the Sevenfold Puja, a poetic sequence of devotional moods, he gives us a feeling for the depth of spiritual practice to be contacted through recitation, making offerings, and chanting mantras.

Knowledge alone cannot take us far along the spiritual path. This book reveals the power of devotional practices to help us commit ourselves to spiritual change with all our hearts.

128 pages
ISBN 0 904766 87 x
£6.99 / $13.95 / €13.95

BODHIPAKSA

WILDMIND

A STEP-BY-STEP GUIDE TO MEDITATION

A Wildmind is as spacious as a clear blue sky, as still as a lake at dawn; such a mind is a source of richness and fulfilment. It is a mind that is free, spontaeous, and abundantly creative. It is a place we can spend the rest of our lives exploring.

This is a guidebook to that inner wilderness. Buddhist meditation teacher Bodhipaksa shows us how we can use simple meditation practices to realize the potential of our minds and hearts.

Wildmind is also an on-line meditation teaching resource at www.wildmind.org

256 pages, with b&w photos
ISBN 1 899579 55 9
£11.99/$18.95/€18.95

MAITREYABANDHU

THICKER THAN BLOOD

FRIENDSHIP ON THE BUDDHIST PATH

This is a book about friendship - about the Buddhist ideals of spiritual friendship and the author's personal experience. By turns moving, funny, and inspirational, Maitreyabandhu's account is as compelling as a good novel. He does not shy away from those crucial and intimate issues that concern us all - aloneness, sexuality, and falling in love.

Maitreyabandhu urges us to place friendship above every other human concern that can be imagined. By the end of this book you might want to do just that.

256 pages
ISBN 1 899579 39 7
£8.50/$14.95/€14.95

PARAMANANDA

CHANGE YOUR MIND

A PRACTICAL GUIDE TO BUDDHIST MEDITATION

Buddhism is based on the truth that, with effort, we can change the way we are. But how? Among the many methods Buddhism has to offer, meditation is the most direct. It is the art of getting to know one's own mind and learning to encourage what is best in us.

This is an approachable and thorough guide to meditation, based on traditional material but written in a light and modern style. Colourfully illustrated with anecdotes and tips from the author's experience as a meditator and teacher, it also offers refreshing inspiration to seasoned meditators.

208 pages, with photographs
ISBN 0 904766 81 0
£8.99/$14.95/€14.95

AKUPPA

TOUCHING THE EARTH

A BUDDHIST GUIDE TO SAVING THE PLANET

This is not just another call to recycle, a litany of destruction, or a bland spiritual homily. Environmentalist and Buddhist teacher Akuppa urges us to see beyond our selfish concerns and wake up to the fragile beauty of the world. This capacity to look beyond ourselves is a seed of heroism. Cultivating this seed, in a thousand ordinary ways, we will find real change is possible after all.

This little book is full of practical advice and profound insight. Jonathon Porritt

128 pages
ISBN 1 899579 48 6
£6.99/$9.95/€9.95